The Long Cold Nights of June

Debby Curreen

Ark House Press
PO Box 1722, Port Orchard, WA 98366 USA
PO Box 1321, Mona Vale NSW 1660 Australia
PO Box 318 334, West Harbour, Auckland 0661 New Zealand
arkhousepress.com

Unless otherwise stated, all Scriptures are taken from the New Living Translation (Holy Bible. New Living Translation copyright© 1996, 2004, 2007, 2013 by Tyndale House Foundation. Used by permission of Tyndale House Publishers Inc., Carol Stream, Illinois 60188. All rights reserved.)

Some names and identifying details have been changed to protect the privacy of individuals.

Cataloguing in Publication Data:
Title: The Long Cold Nights of June
ISBN: 978-0-6483905-9-6
Subjects: Poetry; Grief; Mental Illness; Healing;
Other Authors/Contributors: Curreen, Debby

Design by initiateagency.com

For Hori - we will love and miss you forever.

GEORGE ROBERT CURREEN
22.07.1973 – 6.06.2006

"It is well with my soul."

This collection is dedicated to all of "The Sons of Pariri" —
future, past and present and of course my own sons,
Quanah, Michael, Isaac and Ezra Curreen plus my Grand-Son, Kahu.

Contents ————————————————————•

Introduction ————————•

On a dark Tuesday night in June 2006, my youngest brother took his own life.

He drove out to his favourite beach, parked his car and left us.

I was notified by the police the following day and I had to go with them to make the formal identification of my little brother whose body was now laying cold and silent at the local undertaker.

That day, in an instant my life cracked and I fell into a pit full of never before imagined pain, and a frightening darkness of anguish and confusion.

The grief overwhelmed me and my journey back to a life that was now forever altered, seemed unending.

At times I feared I would never again see the light of another happy day.

My hopes in God, and of course the fierce love I held for my family became my sole purpose for living.

It was at this time that I began to write again as I daily I walked my brother's two beautiful boxer dogs, who were now mine, along the roadside by our home.

I would talk to God, my brother, the dogs and myself, struggling to make sense of suicide and a life that no longer had my beautiful brother in it.

I would go home exhausted and sleep then write my thoughts out.

Gradually life began to settle down and time slowly healed my shattered heart and broken mind.

Many dear friends pulled and pushed me through the darkest times of my life with their love and unceasing belief in me.

I will be eternally grateful for them all.

Grief is messy and unpredictable to manage.

There is no right way to grieve and no magical time frame where you suddenly emerge from a dark tunnel into a bright and happy day.

When a loved one dies through suicide, it is unlike any other grief and is in fact, trauma.

You have nightmares, you cry continually, sleep is elusive and your substance/s abuse becomes infinitely harder to control. I remember going from being a non-smoker to a chain-smoker overnight.

My memory of those first six months is a time of continual chain-smoking and drinking coffee to stave off unpredictable bouts of crying and near screaming.

At night I would drink enough wine or beer to fall asleep, only to wake in the middle of the night crying or gasping from the frightening nightmares that would wake me up.

My hope in sharing my poems of grief, pain, denial, bargaining and hope is that people who have lost loved ones to suicide may be able to relate to my words and that they will help in some way to heal.

The five stages of grief help set a guideline and give you an indication of what you may experience, but once again this too is fluid and the five stages continually swap around inside your head throughout each day.

I have loosely titled each section of my journey, with my own messy "stages of grief".

Eventually, thank God, we do find acceptance and we do move on but we never forget and we never stop missing our loved ones.

All of these stages of grief fade with time and life slowly returns to a different 'normal', but a peaceful one where you can accept your darling's fated decision to say goodbye "on their terms."

And yet even still, after all these years, I will never forget those bitter, sad and lonely cold nights of June 2006 and every June since.

Death and Denial

The Sons of Pariri ———————————•

The clouds gather,
phones ring, hearts break, tears spread
like water on a winter day,
another brother has gone.
As we wait for the moment when,
and we see the crowd part,
as we carry home slowly,
another son from Pariri.
God bless them,
God keep them,
the Sons of Pariri.
I see them in the sunshine, they're laughing loud
and falling all about the house,
and in our lives,
storing up a shelf of memories,
where moth and rust won't eat away,
The joy, the love, you gave and left us,
long gone years and days,
the naughty, daring, darling boys....
our treasured Sons of Pariri.
Whispering behind trees,
I hear all the sons who've gone before us,

3

the still living ones,
striding our road, eating dust with fervour,
the Precious Growing Sons of Pariri.
I wish for a puff of secret cigarette smoke,
and the rattle of ill concealed bottles,
sly grogging on weeknights,
too many sighs to count
and we miss those boys of Pariri.
Brazen strong and glowing,
young gods on their paths, cut short and lost.
But we carried them home
and we bid them farewell,
as our tears washed the road,
where their footprints will always remain and a song plays at night,
serenading whispered goodbyes,
as we join in the chorus…
how we miss them,
our beautiful Sons of Pariri.

FOR NICHOLAS AND GEORGE – You are always home x

Your Death ————————————●

If I had only known that
you believed you were all alone.
If you had told me you were frightened,
I would have come running and brought you home.

Driving through the night and day,
over miles, climbing over rocks,
stepping on nails and glass, poisonous snakes,
to grab your hand,
and dragging you back from the despair inside your head.
Saving you from death.

I wish that you had told me,
you were scared and lonely and sad,
hurting and hating,
your whole entire life.

If only I had found you,
in that last minute before you leapt-
and left me behind.

Would my love be the chord of strength,
that pulled you back home,
and stopped me being all alone.

Life is dark without you.
The life you took from me,
that crushed, and tore, and emptied.

But thank you for the life I had with you.
And thank you for the love,
the joy and fun times, rolling freely together.

The life I now have left is more precious,
Seeing you again one day means everything,
for me, now, death has no sting.

Like Heaven ——————————•

If we were in Heaven,
you would smile,
in a moment before we ran.

Lost in the glow, unshackled;
liberty bouncing all around,
and our hearts would never melt.

A beat, a sigh,
photos almost forgotten
floating by.
If we were in Heaven together,
just for a moment.

I looked up,
but missed your sign;
the one about forever,
and never having to say good-bye.

Give Me A Wish ———————•
to Turn Back Time

Give me a wish,
one just for me,
for a moment in a day;
Please let me turn back,
just one time
in your life.

Let me slip through the window to catch you,
before you turned on me
slammed a locked door,
laying back, closing your eyes,
shutting me out for the last time ...
forever.

Sad Music —————————●

I can't stop myself,
I twist the dial up loud,
till I hear the pain
of sad music.
I post graphic notes,
anonymously on the Internet,
because happy music
 hurts me and stings my broken heart.

Note by note, I fall apart from
the tunes of happy music
because I can't sleep for thinking about you.

I'll die if you never come back into my sight.
Eating, sleeping badly, breathing, sighing,
don't leave me alone.

The please, please, please lamentation
lost adoration,
crushed together,

lost harmonies, hearts and hopes,
cracked dreams.

The sound of sad music lifts me up
and gives me a hope that
perhaps you are still here.

Death in Cars ——————————•

The long cold nights have gone,
spring has come, shadows pass..
the days are long, the sun is out,
flowers bloom.

I have peace at last,
that you have gone.
until I hear of life lost in a car,
tragedy strikes hard.

It blocks the sun,
opens the scars…
and I am back in the trees,
screaming please come back.

The days are long,
the pain too strong,
the death found in cars still remains.

Graves open,
skies cry,
friends gather and I lie alone.

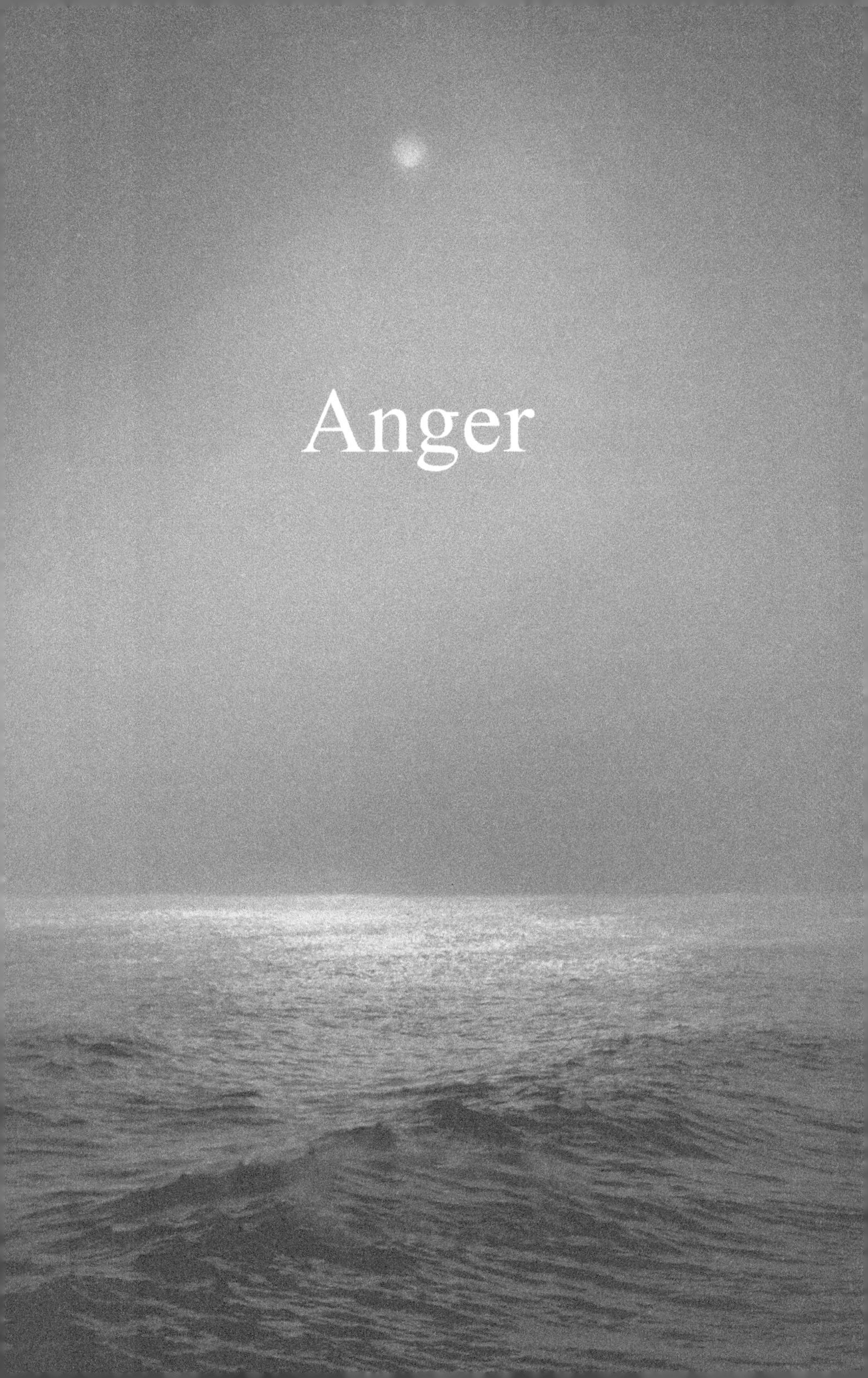

Anger

The Liar's Fire ———————————●

Look at the Liars,
with their pants on fire.
Serves you right, you human blight.

Taint on the horizon,
sty in the eye;
wrecking the day,
with your pork pie lie.

Go reap bad karma! Get hit by a stone!
Live your life with honesty,
leave good people alone.

Look at the Liars with their pants on fire,
shame about the hole in my bucket,
or else I might have saved you –
liar, liar.

Paying Back the ⎯⎯⎯⎯⎯⎯⎯⎯⎯⎯⎯⎯•
Heart-Breakers

I am going to try and think and find a way,
to pay back the heart-breakers;
tear makers, soul aching,
life taker, rats.

Hit where it hurts,
find the spot,
ache and break,
damage a lot.

Pierce the soul,
make those rats shed tears for me.
I am a holder of a ruined heart,
a broken soul; a possessor of
wasted years filled with anger.

Take back my sight,
mop up the sorrow,
patch my soul with love and
squash the rat into the dirt.

I'm going to pay back the heart breakers,
hold my head up, dry my eyes
and hide my heart as I wrap my soul in respect.
Paying back the heart breakers,
living well.

If Only Our Enemies —————•
Left Roses

Man goes to the doctor:
"I am alone in a dangerous world."
Drums roll loudly as a heavy curtain
falls on cruel lips.

Sunrise comes, hallelujah!
Mercies are new every morning –
fear no evil in the shadows.
I have no friends, only Angels.

The thorns on the roses of my enemies
become blunt,
in the falling rays,
of God's bright love.

I Can Wind You Up ————•
Like A Spring

I'd love to wind you like a spring;
up, up and up,
twist, twist, and twist until you break into shouting.
Or you burst into tears.
I don't care.

I would do it to you
because it's funny to watch you fret,
see your face go red,
the tears popping down your mad face as,
you sweat and shriek and get so mad at Me.
Over nothing.

Well nothing that mattered to me,
at least.
Maybe to you.
I just don't care.

I mean, I would really get a kick,
from kicking you,

and making you mad (and sad),
then see you dance with rage.

As the springs inside your head snap
and then your legs would buckle
then bend as your teeth grind.
I know that I should stop.

But gosh,
it would be so damn funny,
to get you wound up over nothing;
that matters to me anyway,
and Mercy seems so scarce today.

Loving Your Enemies ———————•
Too Much

I love my enemies so much,
I am going to buy them all plane tickets
 to far-flung places,
where planes never come back from.

They will ride three legged camels
through the mud of a perishing oasis,
then eat left overs
from condemned restaurants.

Yes, I will bless with plane tickets,
and wave them good-bye;
till later when I have to face the music.

Because God,
I am so much trouble,
for not turning the other cheek.
I should have stayed silent but I chose to speak.

Oh, what's to become of my villainous plans and me?
I will never move forward,
lest I cut out my tongue.

But I'm really going to need it
when it's time to plead,
"Oh mercy me, dear Lord, what have I done?"

Switch the Light Off ──────────●

Say good-bye to sorrow,
close the door on yesterday.

Turn off the light,
the glaring light
where my darkness hides.

Sweep me under the bed,
with all the dust and tears.
Don't try to rescue me,
I am happy with my fears.

Close the door on your way out,
because,
I don't want people to hear my shout;
for the help I don't want,
the comfort that I,
was desperate for yesterday.

No, I'll close my own doors,
and sweep my own dust,
outside.

My bed is the safety net of the dead,
soaked with tears from an aching past;
pillows to be burnt when I am alone,
when you're gone.

I close the door,
and head softly into the darkest tree.

The Dark Night of —————•
Every Man's Soul

There is a dark night,
in every soul,
beneath a slight moon on a long weekend,
far from a family,
left alone beside a beach and out of reach,
of the love that saves,
a man from a fading night.

The sun slides,
friends hide,
guilt rides on the heart of one so alone,
shrouded against the waves of pain,
as the tide rises,
and cries are drowned,
then peace rests in a troubled heart.

Sand trembles as music reaches into the black.
Hearts turn,
memories burn and resolutions fall,

on gentle grass as days roll over into heaven,
goodbyes echo across a mournful ocean,
and the dark night of my beloved's soul becomes still.

Help Me Lord, I Feel Unreal

Colossians 3:10
"Put on your new nature, and be renewed as you learn to know your Creator and become like Him."

Help me God, I feel unreal,
the front that I put up is melting like,
an igloo's doorway in summer,
and the cracks in my armour,
the holes in my mask,
are leaking like a runny nose
in the middle of an important meeting.

But not the meeting I was meant to have with you,
this other meeting,
an approval meeting seeking un- true worth,
with not best friends,
not in any Heaven that can be found on Earth,
certainly not a meeting where I get true love,
not the real stuff,

like God's love in an autumn breeze at twilight,
in that gentle time of refreshments.

I heard a crack, and then a snap,
light rushed in and darkness out;
I heard a shout followed by a yelp,
it was me falling apart a little bit more,
ouch, sore, sniff, sniff, sniff and chunks fell,
ice cold, false hearts, broken masks,
torn apart.
Help me Lord, is this real,
years of pretending starts to peel,
away a pretence too big to bear.
Help me Lord, I'm over here.

Sadness

I Don't Want to Go ——————•
to the Cemetery

Part 1

I don't want to go to the cemetery,
but I will,
and stand by your grave in the cold,
with dying flowers in my hand.

It's lonely and cloudy with no one about,
my flowers will die in the rain.
just like hope did on a grey June day.

I don't want to visit the cemetery,
you're not there,
and I can hum Green Day songs
till I am a basket case.
But I will hope against hope,
and pull you from my memories,
till you laugh out loud,
and all becomes well with my soul.

I will put on some loud music,
pour a drink while you tune your guitar,
then you can play something fast,
and my friends will all dance,
together,
with all of our hearts.
We know you are just missing not gone,
absent, unforgotten,
a pearl of great price,
carried in our hearts,
precious cargo,
waiting at another station.
Resting,
till we all arrive,
glorious, loud and happy to be home,
at last,
with you,
beloved boy, missing brother, loyal friend,
and companion for eternity.
HORI xxx

I Don't Want to Go ———————•
to the Cemetery

Part 2

Fresh Flowers on a Dead Man's Grave
I'm driving through the rain,
off to the cemetery again,
with a bunch of roses,
feeling like some poser,
standing by your grave trying to stop the pain.

Yes it's back to the head stone once more,
try to stop me,
I wish,
right to my core,
it weren't so.
I stand here with our mother,
wishing I could go…
but it is what is and I'm freezing because of you and,
your sudden gone-ness.

So it's back in the rain,
again.
In the middle of winter,
feeling cold,
sad and mad,
wishing you were here and you're not,
fresh flowers on your empty grave,
full hearts, sore eyes and
so, so many, too many.
Good byes xxx

PS. Happy birthday

Crushing the Sleep Stealers ————•

Dark falls,
night stays and feathers ruffle round my head,
as I close my eyes and pray,
the night be not too long.
But thoughts bounce and fingers clench,
a tossed turn with the blankets slipping down,
like the slumber sliding from my soul.

Let's crush the lavender from a thousand fields,
drag bundles across the bed and press my face,
into the potent draught beneath.
For the love of all the pollen in honey ...
I want sleep.

Still, the buds of sleep fall across my pillow,
rolling under the bed,
marbles of disturbance,
blinking in the night cave of my room.
Give me sleep.
For the love of all the whiskey in Ireland.

Rock the cradle.
lullaby me,
soothe me, lie beside me,
till the darkness weakens and
sleep falls
while my hands clench the buds of lavender
from a thousand fields,
and I lie as still as whiskey,
mellowing in an old oak barrel.

If We Were In Heaven ───────────•

If we were in Heaven,
well, just about.
You would smile,
more than a breathe, at me,
just a moment before we ran…

Lost in the glow,
unshackled,
liberty bouncing all around and our hearts would never melt.
A beat, a sigh,
photos, long forgotten
floating by.

If we were in Heaven,
for a moment,
just about,
I looked up,
but missed your sigh,
just about,
and forever,
we would never have to say good-bye.

Shadows Cross ———————————•

I live alone and days cross,
shadows,
hover beyond sunlight and,
then I blink,
as days call me,
forward,
to toss,
and a ghost fades.

Shadows above and laughter falls,
I pick and wonder,
looking behind,
a distant tune, familiar..
humming and a strum but,
there's a gap on the frets.

I cross over,
and behind me shadows dance,
as octaves heighten and I hear,
I think,
I grasp a murmuring speck of dust.
There's a shadow beneath,

a boat of many colours,
and the shadows go,
as I cross.
Good-bye.

But Then It Never ———————•
Goes Away

I spoke on the phone last night,
and my friend we shared our pain.
I told you, there is no closure,
all the rituals,
the pure water sprinkled on aching bodies,
they never change a thing.

Our loved one has still gone.
He will never come back.
We can revisit all we want,
glare at pictures,
beat the air with tired fists and,
and cry till the sun goes down and rises again on another sore day.
Our loved one went away,
nothing changes,
pray.

He won't come back,
kiss the sun,
kick the grave,
pray for help,
make a wish
and say good bye again.

Bargaining

Bury the Chains ————————————•

Can the manacles of a friend passed,
be buried in dust,
ashes blowing,
precious memories crumpling into flames,
on the hearth of home.

Does the mind play tricks with the "light"?
A light that can escape down cracks in old floorboards,
long trodden by love, swept by grace,
danced on with mercy.

Can I throw these off, into the sea of forgetfulness?
Where time swallows pain, and,
then with a waving of farewell,
we drive the dust beneath the wheels of yesterday,
mixing with the ashes,
sighing in the sunshine of all the life
that moves over the seabed of
sunken chains.
Crashing on the shores of tomorrow.

I Should Get Out More ————————•

I must go out more and leave this house,
but the trees and the birds,
beg me to stay behind, just one more day.
My lawn stretches high and flowers pop their petals at the sun.

Where would I go and whom would I see,
to match,
the birds, the trees and me!

The Unbearable ——————•
Light-Headedness Of Un-Being

Unbearably I light my being,
with the sound of your voice,
long gone echoes against the walls
of my heart, yet, bouncing you,
off my soul.

As I begin to un-be,
and myself is unplugged,
so I grasp a stroke of light before
the falls and stumbles,
crack my days, slow my breathe.

I turn my face aside from you
and I break your arms off my life.
Deaf to the light in your eyes,
and mute to your smile.

All I ever wanted,
I wish I could have had,
when I had it all the time,
but the walls of my heart bounced you away.

Dodging Shadows, —————————•
She Laughs

With a dip, she skips,
dodging shadows as a laugh echoes over a heart,
floating in a silent cappuccino,
she laughs,
as her heart bobs softly beneath the foam, from a night of sinking love.
Shadows skim the cup of life,
still,
she laughs, weaving in the light,
her face, chasing the sun,
as the voices call from the emptiness,
where her heart once beat,
but she runs,
and the shadows strain,
the foam melts and she hears a distant whistle,
a beckoning scent on the breeze,
and peace bounces across the meadows.
Her home, her heart, they are safe,
and the sun beams into a brand new cup of life.
For another day, she's dodged the shadows,
she can laugh.

I Hope It All Don't ———————•
Fall Flat

Revelation 4 v 8:

And they chanted night and day, never taking a break: Holy, holy, holy
Is God our Master, Sovereign-Strong? The Was, The Is, The Coming.

There is a hope,
a beat of the heart,
that whispers,
"Lord, may this not fall apart."
The murmurs in the night that cry against hope,
"Please, don't let it all go flat."

The daylight streams,
nights dim,
dreams soar.
What did I ever worry for?
I hear a Holy voice say,
"Carry on through seas of Red,
I've got your back,
Don't turn back,
it won't go flat.

I am here, I am not there,
I am fore you, and behind you.
Don't look back, things won't go flat."

I hear this Holy whisper in the night,
it keeps me going in harsh daylight.
I remember that Holy voice in the dark of night,
saying, "This won't go flat.
Slavery is over, forget about that,
your enemies are drowned,
I turned things around."

I hum in the night,
"things won't go flat,
God's got my back."

So I settle down,
days swim, nights dim,
I wonder,
Holy voices, Godly whispers.
Never in a million years,
hosts of Heaven cheer,
"God's not into flat,
say good bye to all of that.'

Acceptance

Happy Dance, ──────────●
Backward Glance

I swing between the happy dance,
and a backward glance,
a quick look back.

I don't take a chance but,
the music's begun and I see,
friends, I see fun.
There is dancing round and round the mulberry tree,
tonight in my back yard.
We are carefree,
laughing, drinking, talking,
and dancing.

I sweat with joy and laugh with glee,
soaking the sun into the soul of me.
Drinking love,
and breathing friends,
happiness, dancing, may it never end.

I Will No Longer ────────●
Do Penance

No longer shall I do penance,
for the crimes of yesterday.
Nor the expectations of another,
left behind me.

Missed demeaning's,
missed moments,
times healing (over troubled waters) of misted visions,
with unprovoked seconds that blur like stuttering heartbeats.

I won't do penance for misplaced sorrow;
blessings losing richness and,
time won't be unturned.
Only bury my penance under rocks,
heavier than all the words and inactions.

Strike my suffering off your list of want,
leave your rocks of hope on the edge of the undisturbed lake of promises.

Sky Wide, Ocean High ————————•

Grab the dog,
start the car, make some dust, get out far,
because,
it's high tide,
down at the ocean wide,
deep blue,
sparkling ocean,
sky high with love inside.

Give me sunshine,
lose the cloud,
warm the sand and I sigh out loud.
"Woo, this is the life",
as I fall into,
the deep blue sky on the water,
down at the ocean wide,
and I shimmer inside,
with life in the deep blue sea.

I've Mellowed Myself With Merlot

"How does it go?
Are you all right?"
"Yes, I've mellowed myself with merlot."

"Did the day seem too hard and
was sleep lost at night?"
I say, "It's easier with the help of Merlot."

"How is your heart?
Over-hurt and brittle?"
"With sips of Merlot,
things just look little."

"Can you manage well now?
Does you mind turn life over?
Is the past healing now,
are you lying in clover?"

"Sometimes," I say.
"On good days,
I manage.
It was slow.
But I can just get by now, with the help of merlot."

You Should Be Here ————————•

Part I

Today it all comes back,
and you should be here,
all the pictures of you that I run across in my world,
in bleakness, through quiet mists,
where hallways lack laughter,
as our land becomes silent and we wait for,
the first tear to roll,
because,
July 22 is here again,
and you're still missing,
from the day, from my life,
from years and years gone by now and,
still,
I end the day with regret, and I'm sorry.

Part II

The sun lost some of it's light,
many years ago on June 6,
though it was nighttime when you left,

the moon sank a bit lower, and the nights,
oh so cold,
long, dark and empty,
the stillness seeping into our bones,
and the quietness of sorrow,
that will break my heart again and again.
I hate this day,
even now, it hurts too much without you.

Part III

The sun can only rise slowly on July 22,
if we even notice,
or care, as clouds gather closely around us,
holding back comfort and warmth and the
moon moves over a deserted land,
trees muted by our loss.

I wish I could make a joke,
and hear what you would say?
Show me, show me, how and yet,
and yet, so very much,
I know, You would have let me stop you,
if I could have ever heard your cry,
from too far away that night.
I guess we are all so sorry as we raise our glasses one more time,
in silent sadness,
on the longest, coldest night of the year.

Part IV

I refuse goodbyes and yet, still, in the dark I cry out,
"Good bye you stupid egg," and "please,
I wish you could come back",
even though you're happy now,
and you're so far away and I will always love you.
I feel lost and lonely and yet, strange as angels,
it's just a dream.

Diving for Sunshine ─────────────•

Over the bank of a river,
leaning off a platform of happiness,
high above a deep water,
clear and bottomless,
as life escapes for brief moments,
as silence and calm envelopes soul and sunshine,
while we fall,
weightless into the timeless finger tips of infinity.

We hold glee in our mouths,
blowing bubbles into crystalline blue and white,
sinking down below a summer sun,
as clouds guard our backs.
Splash after splash fill the golden air,
bodies dive into the void of an underworld,
the held back joy,
churning below the sparkle,
as hearts rise to the light,
like birth on repeat,
over and over.

Loud breath (es) of shouted joy, and clapping,
exclamations of delight,
as big as new arrivals of life
again and again we jumped.

Can every day be like this?
Quickly touching God.

Hope

Full Moon Shine ———————————•

There's a full moon shine on my lawn and
I'm hiding.
Moon light and star bright,
for lurking in the trees tonight,
there's a promise.

Not a whisper, not a breath,
a sigh of something riding on a whim.
It's the forever after,
strangled laughter,
of love riding the storms.

And it's not the snap of twigs,
or falling cones and leaves.
But the crack of hearts waiting and waiting,
for life.

So turn off the starry night in your eyes,
shun the moon,
stay behind,
dawn's light is just behind the hills.

Miss Spent Sentencing ——————•

Let me miss,
and spend a sentence or two,with you.
Waste a little of your time,
splashing eloquent verse,
in the middle of the day,
when we have nothing better,
than to share a few words,
of love and silly songs.
with coffee, tequila and laughs.

Or did I read that right.
I thought I heard,
and you said,
whilst not quite whispering,
I finish your sentence, half way through the sunshine.
But you were gone,
for a minute,
And then you said.
"Come back."
But I said, "I'm not."
Bye.

You were here.
Oops.

So finish your lines,
with a kiss or a bye,
don't misunderstand me,
with a love or a lie.
See you tomorrow,
I'll write you a note,
sent too soon,
with a missive of love in a sentence.

Smartest Girl on the Planet ———•

It doesn't take a room full of morons to see that,
I'm your Boogie Woo-Man.
Outlaw the bad days and number the sad nights,
and make dreams of picnics in the sun
come true.

Love me,
Invite me.
I'm the smartest girl on the planet.

In your living room,
bring the light,
banish the doom.
I'm you're boogie woogie girl!

Dance the rainbow,
bury the dark.
See you in the morning,
at the picnic in God's Park.

Kind Words ————————————●

I like to bank kind words for bad days.
Save up love,
hoard compliments and cherish moments spent laughing.

Sharing smiles with friends,
and food and wine,
hand poured, home grown-
like friendships we've cultivated over years,
on the vines of life.

I bank kind words,
They accumulate good will.
like (invisible) interest,
love in a mist of memories,
sometimes sown in tears.

Ploughed with sweat,
blood and bone,
flesh joining and sometimes, a life divides;
and trust is buried beneath the blowing leaves of yesterday.

I save up kind words in my heart,
spilling them onto my future.
Growing hope,
bound with strength,
because of you …
every one of you.

Coda

The Long Cold Nights of June ————————•

It's another year.
The days still hang with nights that slow a heart's beat.
Clouds become as big and heavy as the sodden cheeks of mothers,
with the tears that have spilt,
soaking the ground where dogs stand barking.

I beat back the air, stamping my feet,
trying to kill death,
as my screams reach Heaven.
Did you ever hear them?
So loud that they lasted forever,
as I tried to pull you back.
I tried to block the spreading grief,
with all my heart and all my strength,
and every shout of, "No! No! No!"
laying on your body,
looking for a trade,
trying to pull you back,

from the cold night and the darkness I couldn't stop,
that blocked your cries from getting back to me.

Now I pray, Heaven keep you.
The dogs stand watching a heavy sky,
tears spilling on a cold night,
and there's still a distant echo of -
" no…no…no…"

The Life After Low Tide ————————•

Romans 1: 20

Forever since the world was created, people have seen the earth and sky.
Through everything God made, they can clearly see his invisible qualities--his
eternal power and divine nature. So they have no excuse for not knowing God.

The life that I found after low tide,
when waves roll out and weeds sway,
in a falling sea,
beneath a puzzled sky, all wonderful and original images
alone on rocks,
far, far away,
from a wet, and clinging sand.
I share struggles with gravity and moonlight,
waiting out nights and begging for dawn,
like the strains of adoring hymns sung to God.

The sun came,
and dried up all the sand,
water moved over rocks and pushed me up,
so now I stand,
begging seas roll over some old salty tears from yesterday,
show me life between tides,

take me away from the morbid bareness of naked rocks,
like the crescendo of an opera closing.

I sit, not really all sad and alone,
just glad of a life that I have after the biggest low tide,
gone out to sea and never coming back,
like the happy ending of a rock'n'roll medley.

Low tides don't scare me,
not any more because the high one closely follows,
that out to sea,
far from me, but coming back again,
just wait,
like a heavy metal solo,
ringing joy across the waves,
like free access to God,
echoing in the stadium of hope.

Hori and I - December 1999

Acknowledgements ————————————•

Writing a book is like raising a child; you need a village of
support, wisdom, knowledge, encouragement and so much love
and help from your bestie friends and proud sons who tell you
that you are great and that they are proud and impressed.

To the many have had said, "What's stopping you" and "I can't wait to
read/buy your book", "You deserve this", "Would you just hurry up and
publish a book!" and finally the many who said, "You are a really good
writer!"

Thanks.

With a humble and grateful heart, I say, "Thank you so very, very much
to all who have pledged money so that this book could go to print".

God bless you xxx.

I am great believer in God-given appointments with the right people
to help you on your way through life and the God "set-ups" along the way.

To bring this book to print there have been a loyal bunch of dedicated
"villagers" who have given me advice on everything from publishing, tax,
selling, book launchings, marketing, grammar, cover designs, websites
and so on.

Especial thanks to Marty Clayton-Banfield, Sheryl Ormsby, Angela
Short, Catherine Kerr, Suzi Shine, Sallie Rose, Jenny Pennial, and of
course, my proud, strong and loyal sons, Quanah, Michael, Isaac & Ezra.

Kia kaha boys, the Lord is always with you

All the prayers, love and belief in me have been invaluable.

"For surely I would have lost heart had I not believed to see the goodness of the Lord in the land of the living (again).
Psalm 27:13